# Old LESMAHAGOW

*by*
Tom Affleck

**WRECKED AEROPLANE AT LESMAHAGOW**

On a Sunday in May 1916 almost all of the population of Lesmahagow made their way up Garngour Road to the field above Ellenbank where a biplane had made an emergency landing. Some time later as the pilot took off one of the wing tips caught the roof of the waterworks building and the plane nose-dived into a hollow. A young boy sitting on an embankment nearby was injured by a piece of splintered wood and lay in Glasgow Royal Infirmary for three months. Members of the Royal Flying Corps removed the plane the day after the crash.

First published in the United Kingdom, 1998,
by Stenlake Publishing, Ochiltree Sawmill, The Lade,
Ochiltree, Ayrshire, KA18 2NX
Telephone / Fax: 01290 423114

ISBN 1 84033 026 0

Peter Pelling carried on his watch- and clock-making business until the late 1930s from these premises facing Landykeside. From the end of the last century he maintained the town clock and wound it once a week for the sum of £5 a year. In 1904 he received an extra £2 when it became necessary to wind the clock twice a week; he didn't get another pay rise until 1935 when he was given an extra £3. When he retired at the end of 1936 the job fell to the beadle of the Old Parish Church. The clock is still maintained from a legacy left by the Pelling family.

# Introduction

An unknown poet once wrote:

> You come from Lesmahagow! Oh, man, I aince lived there.
> Of a' the places e'er I saw, nane's seemed to me sae fair,
> For beauty hung around it, and health breathed in the air.

There is almost no recorded history prior to the arrival of the monks who first created a settlement at Lesmahagow, although various finds suggest habitation dating back to the Stone Age. Food vessels and axe heads were unearthed during quarrying at Milton early this century. Burial mounds of an age long past have been found, including an exceptionally large one at Skellyhill. Britons and Picts had settlements at Stonebyres, Black Hill and Dillars Hill; these provided the raw materials for the construction of dry stone dykes at the turn of the nineteenth century.

The real history of the village begins in 1143 when David I granted the church and territory to the Abbey of Kelso, 'in reverence to God and Saint Machut'. The charter drawn up by the king instituted a cell 'for the purpose of receiving the poor and whosoever, to escape peril of life or limb, shall flee to the same cell, or within the four crosses standing round about'. Brokencross and Crossford have been suggested as two of the crosses. South Lodge cottage at Auchtyfardle is known locally as World's End and is reputedly the point where fugitives entered the sanctuary. A cell in ecclesiastical terms applies to a lesser or subordinate religious house – in this case Lesmahagow Priory – a daughter house of Kelso Abbey.

The sanctuary was violated in 1335 when Eltham, Earl of Cornwall and brother of Edward III, marched north to Perth with his invading army, stopping overnight in Lesmahagow. The frightened villagers took refuge in the church but Eltham, believing they had supported Bruce, set fire to the building killing all those inside.

The monks of the Reformed Order of Benedictines or Tyronenes were craftsmen of many skills, and set to on various tasks, training locals and employing them to work with them. Stones from local quarries and trees from plantations were used both to build the priory and to expand living quarters for the monks and other settlers. Land was cultivated, and with work readily available, the population quickly increased. The air, although slightly moist, was cold and sharp, making for healthy living. Confirming the health of the population a report from two centuries ago states that in 1770 at the age of 100 J. Porteus walked to Hamilton and returned on completion of his business; he lived for a further five years.

Ranging from 500 to 1,200 feet above sea level, different areas of the land around Lesmahagow were farmed in different ways by the monks and their workers. On the lower ground, with the soil more suited to pasture, cattle grazed, while sheep filled the hills. Adequate springs ensured an endless supply of water for both people and livestock. Following a few years of pasturage fields were cultivated and oats grown; the river provided the power to drive the mills constructed on its banks at Milton and Craighead.

By the end of the eighteenth century the monks were making education a priority, as well as teaching husbandry and other skills. They set up a school which not only taught the basics of writing and arithmetic, but included English, Latin, geometry and sometimes Greek in the curriculum.

At the turn of the century working conditions improved greatly with the growth of weaving, mainly as a cottage industry. This trade employed many people, who found the wages much better than those paid for working on the land. Landowners and employers started to build some fine mansions which also created further diversity of labour. With their increased earnings the populace enjoyed a much better lifestyle; in 1834 one commentator noted that 'Their style and manner of dress may be said to be rather expensive, the servant girl dressing as gaily as the squire's daughter did thirty years ago'.

As the nineteenth century progressed, so working and living conditions improved. Girls started to receive education with the setting up of a school to teach reading, writing and sewing. The priory had gone, but the skills learned from the monks continued to be used. The district had many acres of poor quality land, but improvements in drainage converted these to more pasture and tillable land. What had been merely tracks became good carriageways enabling better communication with nearby villages. The coming of the railway to Brocketsbrae in 1866 and Lesmahagow in 1905 revolutionised transport, and local people began to travel further afield. Many incomers came to the village bringing new skills and ideas with them.

At the beginning of the twentieth century Lesmahagow folk found employment as fruit growers, sawyers, joiners, builders and blacksmiths. The village had no heavy industry, but was used by nearby communities such as Coalburn, Blackwood and Kirkmuirhill for shopping, and a healthy trading community developed. Other workers travelled to shops and offices in Larkhall, Hamilton and Glasgow, while those in the mining industry went in the other direction to Coalburn and Douglas Water. There were coal and ironstone mines in the vicinity, and limestone was also quarried locally.

With the closure of pits after the last war a factory producing hosiery and knitwear became Lesmahagow's principal employer. It has now closed and small units at Milton and Turfholm, with a larger factory at Gateside, are all that remain.

The priory gradually fell into ruin and was finally demolished after the Reformation. In 1978 an archaeological dig revealed its foundations, and these can be seen, with an explanation of their significance, at the south side of the Old Parish Church.

Various suggestions for the derivation of Lesmahagow's name have been put forward. *Lis* or *les* meaning a green or garden, combined with the name of the titular saint St Machut, seems a plausible derivation. No records give a conclusive explanation, however.

Lesmahagow's viaduct was built at the turn of the century, and the house at the foot of the embankment disappeared about this time. Rock excavated to form the cutting for the railway a little to the south was transported in bogies to help build the embankment and fill in the pillars of the viaduct. The land in the foreground, along with what is now Craighead football field, was the 'meadow' of Milton Farm. The collection of farm buildings (centre) developed from a single storey coaching house which stood on the main north-south road from Glasgow to Carlisle. In the twenties the land behind Milton Quarry (background) was developed as Milton Park housing scheme. A new dwelling house for the farm was built on the outskirts of the scheme, and some of the old steadings at Milton pulled down and replaced by Milton Terrace and Milton Place.

Milton Quarry operated for over thirty years, initially supplying stone for local building work, although with the opening of the railway a hundred yards away it could easily be transported outwith the district. The quarry ceased to be worked in the 1920s when the supply of stone was exhausted. Having lain empty for twenty years, the site was used as a bus depot. About the same time as the quarry closed a creamery opened nearby, although it shut prior to the last war when the premises served as a mess for soldiers billeted in the village. A spice packing firm set up business in the building for a period; it was later used by a joinery firm for storage before being demolished.

BROCKETSBRAE STATION.

The first railway line to serve Lesmahagow also had stops at Netherburn, Tillietudlem, Auchenheath and Brocketsbrae, before terminating at Coalburn. The line opened on 1 December 1866, and the station at Brocketsbrae (above) was called Lesmahagow. A horse-drawn brake, carrying passengers to and from the trains, plied between Brocketsbrae and the village.

A new line running through Larkhall, Stonehouse, Blackwood and Lesmahagow opened on 1 June 1905 and joined the old line at Auldton Heights. Twin tracks were laid at Lesmahagow with the intention of having 'up and down' platforms, but the second platform never materialised. The goods yard or 'lie' was busiest during the summer months when tons of soft fruit and tomatoes were despatched to the Glasgow markets. Originally owned by the Caledonian Railway, the line continued to be known as 'the Caley' when it became part of the London, Midland and Scottish.

The opening of the railway made travel to bigger towns and cities easy, and trains ran from early morning until late at night, with special fares for off-peak travel. Passenger services ceased in October 1965, although the line was used to transport coal from Coalburn for a few more years. The station road had an avenue of trees – among them chestnut, beech, aspen, willow, sycamore and silver birch. In June 1967 Lesmahagow station was badly damaged by fire and subsequently pulled down. Houses have since been built on the site; the goods yard has made way for the new High School.

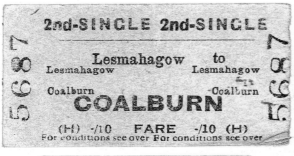

Passengers about to board the last train to Coalburn on 2 October 1965. Four ladies from Milton Terrace can be identified (left to right): Mrs Annie Smith, Mrs Porter, Mrs Smith's mother Mrs Mary Thomson, and Mrs Ellen Affleck. The last-named was making a return journey, having travelled from Coalburn to Lesmahagow when the first train ran in 1905. The gentleman with the soft hat and umbrella is Mr Willie Laird, retired manager of Auchenheath Co-operative.

The blacksmith's workshop on Smiddy Brae was demolished many years ago, although the memory of it lingers on. Standing at the door was like watching a play unfold: the smith with his leather or moleskin apron standing at the anvil, the roar of the fire as he pumped the flames into life, the rhythmic clang of metal on metal, the hiss of steam when the red-hot horseshoe went into the cooling trough. In the days of swing ploughs, harrows and scythes six men worked around an equal number of fires until late at night. It took two men and a boy an hour and a half to make and fit a set of shoes at a cost of 4/- in 1919. The new bungalows of Pathfoot Smiddy now occupy the site of the workshop. (The original Pathfoot Smiddy was a group of cottages called Rotten Row, one part living quarters, the other part workshops, located on the main Carlisle road).

Craighead Mill stands as a ruin, badly damaged by vandalism. Several proposals for its restoration have been put forward, but none has come to fruition. The monks operated two mills, Craighead, built in the thirteenth century and Milton, which was probably older. The latter was demolished almost fifty years ago. Craighead's cellar, with vaulted roof and keyed-in stones, is possibly part of the original building. The mill ground oats for local consumption, but in its heyday 'Oatmeal from Lesmahagow' was also shipped all over the world. Replacement cogs for the great wooden wheel were fashioned from hawthorn, readily available on the banks of the Nethan. Even with the installation of electricity for lighting in 1926 the wheel continued to be worked by water. The electricity was generated from a dam above Craighead football pitch on the Galrig Burn, commonly known as the Balgray Burn. When the mill ceased production in 1975 the same family had owned and worked it for four generations.

Milton Toll, Lesmahagow

This row of four houses was once occupied by mine rescue workers. A garage at the end of the terrace housed their Albion van, nicknamed the Road Louse and governed to a maximum speed of 25 mph – although with a little doctoring it could travel faster. The men trained in pits throughout Lanarkshire and at headquarters in Coatbridge. To get realistic conditions of working in the dark in a confined space they crawled under their own houses, entering through a trap door in the office floor. The squad was disbanded more than sixty years ago, but the houses are still known as the rescue station. They were scheduled for demolition in the 1930s to allow widening of what at the time was the main Carlisle road. The tenants moved, but plans changed and the new road took a different route.

Milton Toll, Lesmahagow

JV 75290

In December 1925 the Parochial Lodging House, known as the 'puirs hoose', had an average of thirteen residents, housed at a weekly cost of 8/3. By the thirties the building had become a private dwelling. It served as a billet for army officers during the last war and was finally pulled down in 1974 to make way for a slip road. The toll house, on the other side of the road, was demolished in the fifties. Some years after this picture was taken Belisha beacons for a pedestrian crossing were put up just where the pavement starts. Craighead Farm is in the background.

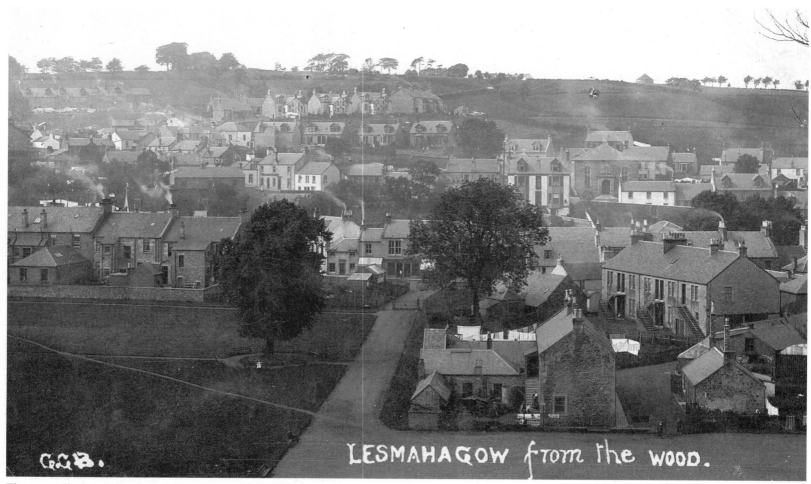

LESMAHAGOW from the WOOD.

This overall view takes in the central part of the village and New Town, much of which fell victim to post-war planning. Among the demolished property in the foreground is two-storeyed Woodview, with the old church school behind – the school finished its days as a joiner's shop. The shops on Main Street visible between the trees have been replaced by a car park. The Mound is in the centre, with Cordiner church to the right (both now gone) and Greenfield House to the right of that. Houses in Bankhouse Road, Beechwood Crescent and New Road are clear in the background. The Masonic hall, which was built at the park entrance, did not appear until later in 1927.

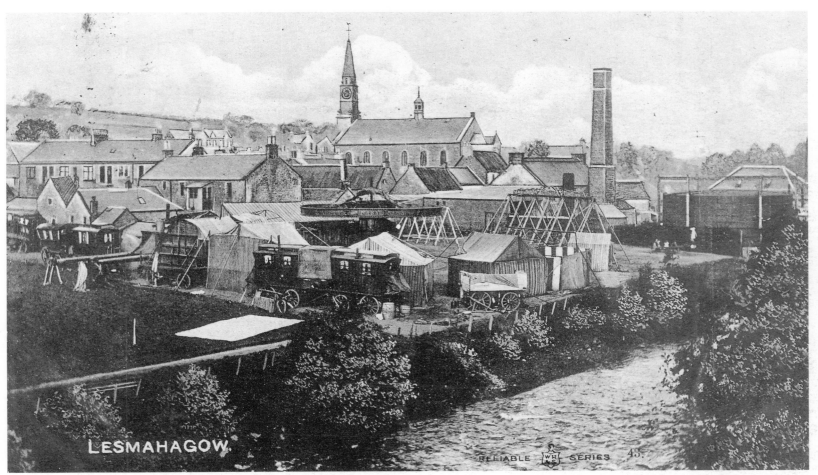

LESMAHAGOW.

RELIABLE [WR] SERIES 43.

The travelling fair visited Lesmahagow regularly; this picture shows it pitched next to the gasworks on what later became the putting green. Its presence was normally associated with the hiring fairs, held in the square on the south of the church, when men and women hoping to improve their lot bargained with farmers and estate owners for a position which bettered those they held. Wages agreed, a few shillings changed hands and the workers tried their lot at the fairground attractions. Children newly out of school also found work through the hiring fairs which continued well into this century. The first moving pictures came to Lesmahagow with the fairs. Travelling showman, Freddie Palmer, showed his silent films in a tent; he eventually settled in Lesmahagow and built a permanent picture house.

The Mackirdy Fountain stood at the junction of Main Street and New Trows Road, and despite having been gone for over seventy years that part of the village is still called 'fountain'. When buses first operated to Lesmahagow in 1925 the drivers complained that they did not have enough room to turn and the fountain was removed shortly afterwards. It's not known what happened to it, although it is believed it may have been broken when it was dismantled. The photo shows all the paraphernalia of boilers, engines and roller ready to tar the road for the first time – perhaps a good opportunity to remove the fountain.

Gas came to Lesmahagow in 1845 and gas street lighting had been installed by 1860. During the summer months the shades were removed for cleaning and stored along with the mantles, a practice which continued until the last war when the village, like the rest of the country, had no illumination summer or winter. Another boon to the householder was the arrival of a piped supply of water, which was laid on from the top of Spoot Brae at Fountainhead, after tests proved the spring there to be of the highest quality. The trek up the hill for water became a thing of the past.

LESMAHAGOW

A scheme to widen the road from the bottom of Main Street to the Royal Bank was planned and approved in the late 1930s, although the war put a stop to the work and nothing happened until the cessation of hostilities. A return ticket to Glasgow with the SMT cost 2/9 for many years and well into the fifties. With a service every half hour – and the expansion of the village away from the railway station – taking the bus became more attractive and ultimately led to the closure of the railway. The early days of bus travel saw various operators, including Glasgow Omnibus Company (GOC), A1 and XL, although these all eventually merged into Scottish Motor Traction Company. Gushet House is in the centre of the photo, with Shand Terrace and Wellbank up the hill on the right at Peasehill.

Young's shop stood at the corner of Main Street and the south side of Landykeside with the printing works next door, the latter now a garage and the shop a cafe. As well as carrying out printing work and selling stationery, newspapers and periodicals they advertised fancy goods, china, local views and comic postcards, tobacco and cigarettes. Those with a taste for music were not forgotten with the sale of violin and banjo strings, gramophones and an audition room for hearing records before purchase.

19

Before the days of easy travel Lesmahagow could claim to be a self-supporting community. John Rowe's tailor shop (opposite) stood half way up Bakers Brae – on Main Street there were Tom Brown and Brown & Scott – all employed large staffs.

Other traders in Lesmahagow included at least four boot and shoe shops, two milliners, five drapers, five bakers, a saddler, six grocers, an ironmonger selling everything from a small nail to rolls of fencing wire, and five hotels catering for the travelling salesmen. Several of the tradesmen toured the district as 'packmen', carrying samples of their wares to outlying areas. These traditional trades have all but disappeared.

Coalburn and District Co-operative, referred to as the C&D, thrived in Lesmahagow until dissent arose in 1912 with locals on the board wanting to break away and form a Lesmahagow Co-op. A large crowd gathered outside to hear their views and the outcome was the formation of Abbeygreen Co-operative Society further along the Main Street, at the north corner of Landykeside, in 1913. The shops competed with each other, both stocking a wide range of goods until the collapse of the C&D in 1930. An abiding memory of the C&D for some ladies was the wonderful sale of clothing after the 1927 flood. The shop had a unique distinction – its phone number was Lesmahagow 1. Hope Hall and the Post Office now occupy the premises.

The Coalburn branch of the Abbeygreen Co-op has closed, and the Lesmahagow shop now only sells groceries. The society had a hall above this shop, and owned extensive land and premises in Landykeside including a large bakery, stores and stables. As their need for these declined they were sold off; they now house cars, vans and council equipment. During the last war the Home Guard used one of the upstairs rooms in the outbuildings as its headquarters. The Glebe Cinema stood on part of the land for 30 years. It showed its last film in September 1961 and its site is now a car park.

Examples of transport at the end of the last century, with two delivery carts on the left and a carriage outside the Commercial Hotel. The British Linen Bank lost its railings in the scrap metal drive during the last war; its trees were cut down many years ago. The shop in the right foreground, Brown and Scott's tailors, later had a second storey built on to it. After Brown and Scott gave up trading the ground floor was occupied by Pelling, grocer and tea merchant, who moved from smaller premises across the street. Beyond the Commercial Hotel are shrubs which lined that part of the street before the building of shops and houses.

The Royal Hotel (left) and the adjoining building on its far side have now been replaced by the library. The Royal was previously called Stoddart's Sun Inn and hired out carriages which were kept on the ground floor of the building at the rear; stabling was on the first floor, and access for the horses was by ramp. At one time an outbuilding behind the Commercial Hotel (right) housed a weaving shed. The shop nearest to the camera on the left was a jenny-a'-things; the next one along was Cairncross & Menzies the ironmongers. The middle window of the Commercial Hotel is now wider and in the 1930s was converted to an oriel – this later had to be removed as it caused an obstruction for larger lorries.

A joy wheel first turned in the public park at the beginning of the 1930s, and judging by this picture it seems to have brought joy to young and old on its first day of use. Later in the day many anxious mothers made their way along the road to find out why their offspring had not arrived home from Turfholm School, only to find them on the packed wheel and unable to get off. Along with the maypole in the background and the chute, the joy wheel was subsequently removed on the grounds of being dangerous. The man on the extreme right is local builder Willie Fairservice who laid the cement.

GOSPEL HALL DRIVE, LESMAHAGOW.

The local Hope Hall Assembly was founded in 1865 and originally met in Miller's joiner's shop at the foot of Old Brae, the sawdust swept aside to make way for the communion table. With more room required they moved to Brown's Land in New Town, now known as Calsay Knowe. The movement grew from the first meeting of five people to an assembly of nearly 100 in 1875, with large meetings held outside. Then James Anderson erected a two storey building which accommodated his drapery on the ground floor and provided a 300-capacity hall upstairs. A great annual event, the Hope Hall Drive was a children's trip, well attended by adults too. Just prior to the turn of the century as many as 370 joined the cavalcade of a three horse charabanc, eleven three horse brakes and one two horse brake, all followed by a local baker with his horse-drawn van carrying the provisions for the outing.

How comfortable transport was almost 100 years ago is hard to tell, but this group from the Parish Church choir seem to have arrived at Loudoun Hill safely, and no doubt glad the rain stayed off.

28

A group of Lesmahagow people at the Toll Corner, off for a day's outing to St Mary's Loch in the luxury of an early 1920s touring bus, the *Julian*, with apparently no limit to the number of passengers. McRae & Haldane who owned the bus had a coachbuilding company at Bloomfield and sold and hired vehicles. In later years the McRae family operated modern touring buses.

*Mr. Samuel Park's Garage*

Robert Park started his motor mechanic's business at Portland Cottage, Springbank and his two sons, Sam and Bob, later had their own businesses. Sam's premises (above) stood on the west side of the Carlisle Road at the top of the Smiddy Brae. With the coming of the dual carriageway in 1938 another filling station was built on the southbound side of the road. This 1930s photo shows an Overland with wooden-spoked wheels, an Austin 12, and a Morris van presumably driven by the butcher standing beside the mechanics.

Bob Park's garage stood in the New Trows Road and consisted of three large wooden buildings, two of which still stood until recent years. Now there is only one and it is due for demolition soon. Over the years these buildings have housed various vehicles including a hearse, taxi, and during the last war the AFS fire engine which was driven by one of Bob's daughters. For many years one of the sheds bore a large sign for the Salvation Army, who had used it in the 1920s.

It looks as if the entire population of Turfholm turned out dressed in their Sunday best for this photograph. The date is unknown, but a surprising feature is the wire leading from the telegraph pole into one of the houses – phones in working class homes were almost unknown until well into this century. The roofs in many of Turfholm's sixty houses had rafters that were neither straightened nor dressed, but just as they were cut from the trees. One young visitor referred to his uncle's dwelling as the house with the garden in the roof, for often weeds grew among the thatch. The four-classroom school stood behind the railings on the far right and children spent their Saturday penny across the road at Granny Gibson's shop on the corner of Rowe Street. Only a few of the houses, now modernised, remain to show the old character of the Howm.

A soup kitchen has been part of village life on several occasions in times of hardship, such as the miners' strikes of 1921 and 1926 and the Depression of the 1930s. Soup and potatoes formed the main fare and men helped the women in the preparation of the food. When the soup kitchen was in operation in 1921 the *Hamilton Advertiser* reported that 'Mr Freddy Palmer's Picture Palace gave a performance which, including his donation, raised £14.3.6d for the fund'. The location of this kitchen is believed to have been Turfholm.

LESMAHAGOW FLOOD
HAVOC
BIRKWOOD BRIDGE

Lesmahagow Parish suffered from flooding on several occasions. In 1920 at least five bridges over the Nethan were swept away and several houses in the Turfholm area were extensively damaged – a dramatic group raised £30 for the victims. The worst flood came in July 1927 when a cloudburst swelled small burns to extraordinary volumes. The cemetery wall collapsed and some of the newly erected houses at Milton Park were flooded. Five inches of water swilled around a house at Milton Terrace. The worst of the damage, however, was caused by the Kilnhall Burn which brought great quantities of debris down in its flooded waters. It destroyed Sandknowe Bridge, blocked the culvert at Rookwood and poured along the road, filling Main Street with hundreds of tons of boulders and tree stumps and leaving shop premises and ground floor houses deep in mud. After this disaster the Kilnhall Burn was diverted away from the culvert and into the Nethan across from the bowling green.

When the Hon. James Hozier MP laid the keystone of the arch over the doorway of the Parish Church Hall in 1902 he did so with 'a unique antique trowel suitably inscribed'. A large gathering turned out to see the ceremony, conducted in Masonic style, and to hear speeches from the various dignitaries and listen to the praise led by the church choir. The trowel recently turned up at an auction in the Midlands, valued by a London silversmith at £4,000.

Scottish Quoiting Association Challenge Cup, Won by Lesmahagow Q.C.

The great miners' sport of quoiting was at its height between the two wars and Lesmahagow had an enthusiastic club. The local quoiting 'green' (the ground was in fact bare) was situated on the east side of the Nethan just beyond the Gasworks' Brig. Crowds larger than those that first and second division football clubs attract today watched and cheered exciting games. These often continued on into the darkness when the man at the clay, displaying the ultimate in faith, sparked a match and held it over the paper marker, guiding his team-mate to the pin. Large sums could be won in prize money, and from side bets. Lesmahagow had many excellent players who gained several trophies; their top achievement was winning the Scottish Association Challenge Cup in 1924. For this each man received a gold watch, presented by local MP, Tom Dickson.

Five-a-side football was a huge attraction for players and spectators earlier this century. At the annual cattle show as many as 100 teams entered a tournament, the early rounds of which were played on a Saturday and into the following week, with the final on the Wednesday. Two of the best known teams were the Gordons and Famous Five who won countless trophies around the district. The team associated with the Shankly brothers, the Glenbuck Cherry Pickers, generated great rivalry among competitors, but Lesmahagow could hold their own. Many of the fives players went on to senior careers – Garrett to Hearts, Forrest to Clyde, Telfer to Albion Rovers, Williamson, Waddell and Grierson to Preston, and Fallow to Lancaster. Eleven-a-side teams also competed, first in juvenile leagues and later as juniors. When Nethanvale Thistle lost their ground for house-building at Milton Park several venues were used, among them Bogside, Devonburn and Woodhead, where Lesmahagow played before finding a permanent home at Craighead Park.

Cyclists from Lesmahagow and Coalburn. To balance on a penny farthing long enough to have a photo taken was quite a feat. Some of these bikes were stored in the blacksmith's at Smiddy Brae, and when the small wheel came off one and a replacement could not be found the smith fitted a wheel from an old lawnmower, although it didn't prove successful. Older members of the community will remember the penny farthing on the roof of another smiddy at Bereholm. About fifty years ago it found a new home in Troon.

Birkwood estate made land available at Turfholm for a bowling green and a club came into being in 1879. This photo, taken during the First World War, shows members and wives dressed for opening day in front of the old clubhouse. Included in the group are some of the wounded soldiers from Auchtyfardle hospital. The club has enjoyed success during its long history, not only in local competitions, but further afield, counting national champions and international players among its members. A Lesmahagow man, Robert Barrie, secretary of Lanark bowling club, became President of the International Bowling Board in 1964.

During the First World War Auchtyfardle House became a hospital for the wounded. This picture shows nurses and men from various regiments at the entrance to the house.

This part of the New Town has gone completely, with modern housing now built on the west (left) side. The house just visible on the right was Peppermint Cottage, with the Mound beyond it. Originally one dwelling with a large terraced garden to the rear, it was refurbished as four separate houses after being gutted by fire. The two storey building to the left was officially called Bellview Terrace but was nicknamed Honeymoon Terrace as so many newly-weds set up home there. Adjoining it was Viaduct View with shop attached. It too fell victim to fire, then saw service as a coal yard, finally becoming the garage for the fire engine prior to the opening of the new fire station at Carlisle Road. Cordiner Church stood behind the gate with the light. It closed in 1941 and later served as a small factory for the manufacture of crisps and as a dance hall, both for short periods. The church is remembered by the new houses named Cordiner Court. The Templar's Hall was just beyond the water pump; Peasehill Cottage stands at the end of the road.

Nothing brings back memories of past times more aptly than a picture of a man and his horses ploughing. Although the image conjures up peace and tranquillity, in a muddy field in wet and windy weather it was a cold, thankless task for the ploughman. Working a normal day he could plough an acre, equivalent to about four rigs, depending on the length of the field. In addition, he had to feed and groom his horses and harness them up for work. Nowadays a tractor with as many as eight furrows will work well over twenty acres in a day and can plough on slopes impossible for the man with horse-drawn equipment.

Hay making was a back-breaking job. The reaper cut the hay which then had to be turned. When it had dried sufficiently it was gathered into small bundles called kyles for easier handling before building the rick. All tasks were carried out with a pitchfork. Later, by means of a roller system of ropes or chains and hand-turned wheel (above) the rick was hauled on to the lifter and moved to the farmyard for building into stacks or storing in the large hay shed. It took a squad of ploughman, byreman, general labourers and temporary workers many days to complete the tasks in providing fodder for wintering the animals. All this hard work has now been mechanised and the grass is either baled as hay or turned into silage.

One of Lesmahagow's 'big hooses', Birkwood is a relatively modern structure which was built in 1856, despite its castellated architecture. Many fine works of art adorned the walls and two letters written by Prince Charles in 1745, along with one of his brooches, were among the treasures in the house. A wing was added in 1890 for the expected visit of the Queen of France; South Lodge and avenue were constructed some years later for another visitor, the Grand Duke Michael of Russia; neither visit ever took place. A further addition, the avenue and bridge over the Nethan, gave easier access to the village through Turfholm. The Mackirdy family who lived in Birkwood donated £1,000 to the cost of the public park in 1901 and members of the family are remembered by a stained glass window and baptismal font in the Old Parish Church.

Birkwood went up for auction at the Trades' Hall in Glasgow on 29 September 1920 and was bought by Lanarkshire County Council to become a hospital for the mentally handicapped. The particulars of sale listed 18 bedrooms, 7 public rooms, picture gallery, gun room, nursery, 3 entrance halls, strong room, wine cellar, laundry, various amenity rooms and extensive servants' quarters. The grounds contained a large walled garden, peach house, tennis court, curling pond, stables and many workers' cottages. In addition a shooting moor and many farms and houses in the village belonged to the estate, which was originally the property of the monks.

In December 1904 W.A. Scott Mackirdy, owner of Birkwood, completed the organisation of a private fire brigade to protect his mansion and estate buildings. A year later, *Fire and Water* reported that 'So far no serious fire at Birkwood Castle has put the Brigade to the test, but the men are thoroughly enthusiastic and smart in handling the steamer and hose'. The nine estate workers who doubled up as firemen were equipped with an 'up-to-date light 200-gallon' fire engine and were subjected to regular drills and test alarms to ensure their capability for the job.

On 16 August 1905 the brigade got the opportunity to tackle a real fire at a row of cottages in Lesmahagow. Mr Mackirdy's son, in charge of the brigade, reported that 'Although the fire had got a good hold . . . in a few minutes we had the pleasure of seeing that we had the fire under perfect control'. The team got to the scene of the fire eleven minutes after the alarm was raised.

During the summer months working 'oot bye' provided a source of pocket money for a generation of schoolchildren and often a very welcome extra for hard-pressed housewives. There were fields of strawberries, redcurrants and gooseberries at Brocketsbrae, New Trows and Kerse. A disease almost wiped out the strawberry growing industry in the 1920s. However, with the advent of disease-resistant varieties it gradually picked up. The Kerse horn was not only a reminder to the workers at Kerse of starting and stopping times; mothers told their children to 'come back home for your dinner when you hear the horn'. Other workers travelled to the fruit-clad fields of Clydeside by Hammy's bus or bike; in the 1930s a boy or girl could earn about 6d an hour. This work has now gone, and the few remaining strawberry fields advertise 'pick your own'. The photo shows a group of young women and girls, rather well dressed for the work, and two boys with the fruit grower, possibly at Brocketsbrae.